People go underground, too. Here are some of the reasons why. They may go to:

- use road and rail tunnels
- dig up coal, gold and diamonds
- explore caves for fun!

An underground train.

A miner going underground to work.

Rabbits spend time above ground and underground.

3

Desert meerkats

Meerkats are desert animals that live in groups called gangs.

AFRICA

Kalahari
Desert

Meerkats live in the Kalahari Desert, which is in Africa.

Going Underground

Contents

John Malam

OXFORD

Under your feet

Did you know that there is a whole world under your feet?

If you were an ant, a worm or a mole, you would spend most of your life under the ground. There's even a bird that makes its nest underground, not in trees or bushes. Animals go underground for lots of different reasons.

They may go to:
- look for food
- rest and sleep
- make nests and have their young
- escape from danger
- keep warm or keep cool.

Moles can dig 20 metres of tunnel a day!

Q: How do you stop moles from digging up your garden?
A: Take their spades away!

Meerkats dig underground **burrows**. The burrows are safe places where they give birth to their young. They sleep in their burrows at night. In the daytime they leave their burrows and set off in search of food. When meerkats are in danger, they run to their burrows to keep safe.

At the start of the day, meerkats stand outside their burrow. They face the sun to get warm.

A day in the life of a meerkat

1 In the morning, meerkats come out of their underground burrow to find something to eat.

2 Meerkats eat worms, grasshoppers, lizards, snakes, scorpions, eggs and fruit. Most of all, they love **grubs**!

3 When it's really hot, they have a nap. One meerkat stays awake and looks out for danger.

4 The look-out sees an eagle. Eagles eat meerkats! The look-out calls out and everyone hides in the burrow until the eagle goes away.

5 Now the meerkats are looking for food again. Will anyone find a big fat grub?

6 At bedtime the meerkats cuddle up inside their burrow. Goodnight, meerkats!

Q: How do meerkats eat snakes?
A: Very carefully!

Ant antics

Ants are amazing insects! Let's follow some busy worker ants under the ground.

Most ants live in a group or colony in an underground nest. The nest has lots of galleries (tunnels) and chambers (rooms).

Here's what worker ants do:
- dig new galleries and chambers
- keep the nest tidy
- collect food
- take food into the nest
- look after the eggs and the larvae (grubs)
- keep enemies away.

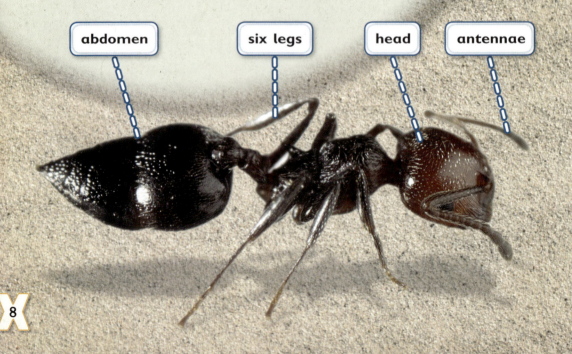

abdomen   six legs   head   antennae

Life inside an ants' nest

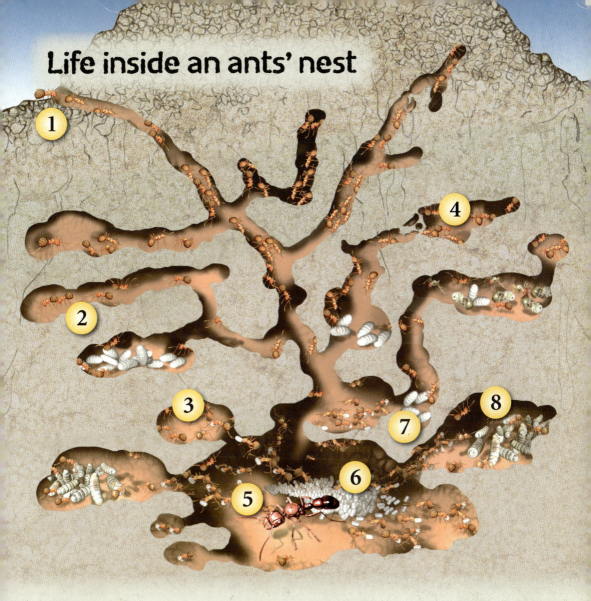

Key

1 Entrance tunnel
2 Gallery
3 Chamber
4 Worker ants
5 Queen ant
6 Eggs
7 Larvae
8 Cocoons

Ant life-cycle

2

Worker ants take the queen's eggs and put them in chambers.

1

A special ant lives deep inside the nest. This is the queen ant and it's her job to lay eggs.

Q: What is the biggest ant in the world?
A: An eleph-ant!

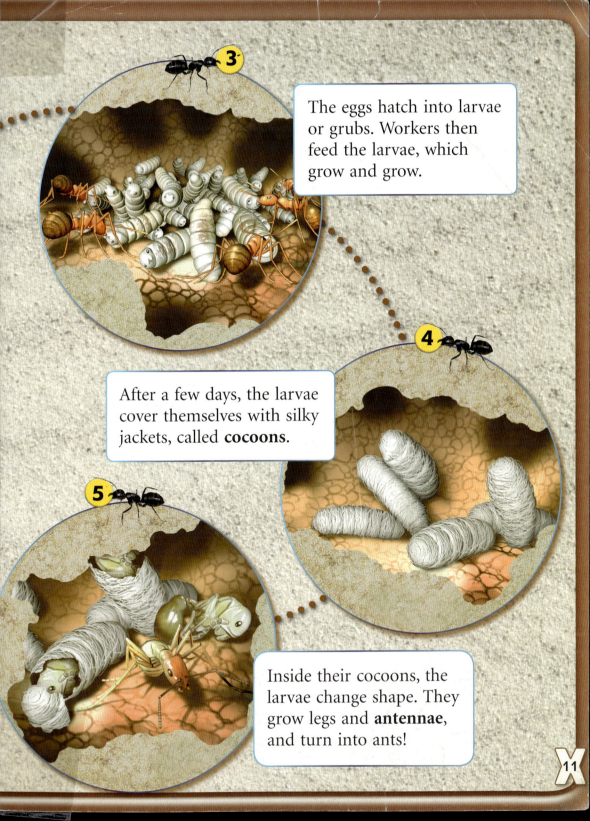

3 The eggs hatch into larvae or grubs. Workers then feed the larvae, which grow and grow.

4 After a few days, the larvae cover themselves with silky jackets, called **cocoons**.

5 Inside their cocoons, the larvae change shape. They grow legs and **antennae**, and turn into ants!

Bird in a burrow

Seabirds often make their nests along the coast, on bare rocks or between tufts of grass. But the puffin makes its nest under the ground.

Each spring, puffins dig burrows. Sometimes they use old rabbit burrows. The burrow is a tunnel, about two metres long. An egg is laid at the end of the tunnel where it is safe.

The male and female puffin take it in turns to go underground and keep their egg warm.

After about 40 days the egg **hatches** and out comes a chick. It lives underground until the summer, when the young puffin leaves its nest for the first time. It can't fly, so it tumbles into the water and swims away. Gradually, it learns to fly and fish for itself.

When it is four or five years old, it will dig a burrow and start a family of its own.

Puffins can hold around 10 fish in their beaks at once! They feed some of the fish to their hungry underground chicks.

Into the bat cave!

A cave is a hole under the ground or inside a mountain. Some caves are big, some are small. Even though caves are usually dark and sometimes wet, they are home to many different creatures – from bugs to bats!

Bats are the only **mammals** that can fly!

Q: Why don't bats live alone?
A: They prefer to hang out with their friends!

Bats sleep in caves during the day because they like the dark. They sleep hanging upside down from the ceiling to keep them safe from animals on the ground.

Bats go outside at night to hunt for insects. It is dark when they hunt so they don't use their eyes to find insects, they use their ears. They make a sound and listen for the **echo** of that sound bouncing back off objects around them. This helps bats to find out where insects are and how big they are.

Caves can be home to thousands of bats.

Cave rescue

Think about going into a narrow, wet cave. You'd have to squeeze and crawl along underground passages. Some people do this for fun. It's exciting but it's also dangerous.

A caver lowers himself into a dark underground passage.

A helicopter takes the injured caver away to hospital.

Some people like to crawl into a cave called *Roaring Hole*, in Yorkshire, England. It's a type of cave called a pot-hole, which is a long and narrow **shaft** in the ground. In 2005, a group of cavers lowered themselves into the cave using rope. Suddenly, one of the cavers fell! Then a big rock came loose and fell onto him. It broke his leg. His friends went to get help.

A rescue team arrived and they climbed down to the man. The cave was so narrow that they could not put him on a **stretcher**. Instead, they wrapped his broken leg, then carefully pulled him back up to the surface. It took seven hours to get him out!

Long-lost art gallery

The most famous cave in France was found by a dog! The dog's name was Robot and on 12th September, 1940, it fell into a hole.

Robot's owner, a boy called Marcel, pulled his pet out of the hole. Some stones fell in, and when they landed they made an echo. It sounded like there was a big hole under the ground. Marcel decided to explore it with three of his friends. Carefully, they climbed down and came into a cave.

Marcel shone his torch into the dark and the boys couldn't believe what they saw. Pictures of horses, deer and cattle were painted on the walls! There were more than 600 animal pictures, which were painted thousands of years ago. It was a prehistoric art gallery! No one knew it was there, until Robot's accident. Soon, the whole world knew about the amazing painted cave at Lascaux (say: lass-co).

The painted cave at Lascaux.
Can you tell what the paintings are?

It's an underground world!

Moscow Metro

The Moscow Metro is well known for its beautiful stations. If you get lost, then listen to the announcer's voice. If it is a man then you are going into the city centre. If it is a woman then you are travelling out of town. What a clever idea!

Electric mountain

At Dinorwig, North Wales, a power station for making electricity is hidden inside a mountain. There are lots of long tunnels and huge rooms filled with giant machines. It's a beautiful part of Wales and the countryside has not been spoiled because the power station is out of sight.

Cool living

Matmâta is a village in Tunisia, north Africa. It's very close to the Sahara Desert. People live in cool caves to escape from the heat. Some caves have an upstairs and a downstairs just like a house!

City of the future?

There are lots of animals that live underground.
Can *you* imagine living underground one day?

Japan is a very crowded country. In the future some people might live in a new city built under the ground. It will be called Alice City. There will be plenty of room for everyone. As well as homes, there will be hotels, offices, libraries, cinemas – and schools of course!

An artist's impression of Alice City, Japan.

Glossary

antennae   feelers that grow on the heads of insects

burrow   a hole in the ground that an animal lives in

cocoon   a covering that some insects spin from silky threads to protect themselves while they are changing into their adult form

echo   when you hear a sound again as it bounces back off something solid

electricity   the energy that is used to give light and heat and to work machines

grub   an animal like a small worm that becomes an insect when it is an adult

hatch   when a baby bird or animal comes out of an egg and is born

mammal   an animal that gives birth to live babies and feeds its young with its own milk

shaft   a long, narrow passage in a building or underground

stretcher   a long piece of fabric with a pole on each side used for carrying somebody who is sick or injured

Index

For an exciting underground adventure you can read …

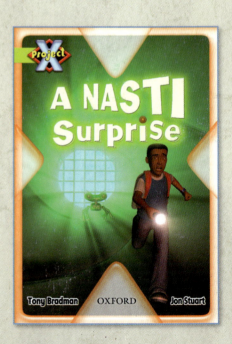

Project X

A NASTI Surprise

Tony Bradman   OXFORD   Jon Stuart